D1163023

THE OWL
QUESTION

May Swenson
Poetry Award Series

THE OWL QUESTION

poems
by

Faith Shearin

UTAH STATE UNIVERSITY PRESS
Logan, Utah

Utah State University Press
Logan, Utah 84322-7800

Manufactured in the United States of America.
Cover design by Barbara Yale-Read

The following poems have appeared previously, sometimes in slightly different forms:

"Entropy," in *Alaska Quarterly Review,*"Counting," in *Amaranth*, "Matrimony," in *New York Quarterly*, "Ruins," "Our Story," and "Alone" in *Ploughshares*, "Innocence," in *The Iowa Woman*, "Luck," and "Lust," in *The Chicago Review*, "Homecoming," in *The Charlotte Poetry Review*, "Piano Lesson," in *Lowell Pearl*, "Rescue," in *Lullwater Review*, "The Unexpectant," in *Provincetown Arts;* "Retriever," "Hunger," and "On Halloween," in *Poetry Northwest*, "Becoming Mother," and "Opera," in *Witness* "Entropy," "Ruins," "Luck" and "Alone" in *The Third Coast Anthology*.

Library of Congress Cataloging-in-Publication Data

Shearin, Faith.
  The owl question / Faith Shearin.
      p. cm.
Winner of the 2002 May Swenson Poetry Award.
  ISBN 0-87421-444-0 (pbk. : alk. paper) — ISBN 0-87421-445-9 (cloth : alk. paper)
  I. Title.
PS3619.H36 O95 2002
813'.6—dc21
                              2002004492

For Tom and Mavis

CONTENTS

ACKNOWLEDGMENTS

THANKS TO THE FOLLOWING PEOPLE AND ORGANIZATIONS FOR THEIR support in this endeavor: Michael Delp, Jack Driscoll, Alan Dugan, Marie Howe, Cynthia Huntington, Thomas Lux, Richard McCann, Thomas Murdock, James Richardson, Lucy Rosenthal, Anne and Norman Shearin, Annie Belle Shearin, Dana Shearin, Will Shearin, John Skoyles, Henry and Ruth Spruill, Melanie Sumner, Michael Spooner and the Utah State University Press, The Fine Arts Work Center in Provincetown, Cranbrook Schools, and The National Foundation for Advancement in the Arts. Thanks especially to Mark Doty.

The Owl Question BEGINS IN EAGER INNOCENCE, A LONGING TO KNOW
the world:

> . . . how will I fit all this life in one life?
> I need a map, a vocabulary list; I can't learn the world
>
> fast enough. I want to be like the girl upstairs who has braced
> herself before a grand piano and taught her own blind fingers to sing.

Faith Shearin's narrative is the story of a sentimental education. But
it isn't all the familiar version, in which a youthful pilgrim learns to see
with increasingly disenchanted eyes. Instead, there's something know-
ing in Shearin's innocence to begin with, and likewise something pere-
nially innocent in her knowing. Experience offers not only "the owl
question" but inescapable others:

> . . . Four formal
> questions in the book that turns a family into trees:
> When did you come? Who did you meet?
>
> Who did you make? How did you fall away?

Eager as the speaker in these poems is to put on the bonds of love,
she knows from the beginning that affections are never uncomplicated,
and that what we desire is also fraught with dangers:

> . . . I imagined I could try on wife like
> a fake fur coat and the way I looked in it would
> make me laugh. Instead, wife was like gaining
> fifty pounds, all on my ass, or waiting for bad news
>
> from a doctor.

What she wishes, wisely, is to be able to love and to see clearly at
once. She understands that to do so will require all her resources: irony,
good cheer, truthfulness, humor, and a carefully preserved attention to
the strangeness of living, the peculiarity of all our enterprises. The
result is a lovely, trustworthy first book, full of affection and wry clarity,
"all life's finite hope leaning closer for a kiss."

Mark Doty

THE OWL
QUESTION

You did, you loved, your feet
are sore. It's dusk. Your daughter's tall.

Thomas Lux
(from The Drowned River*)*

The masseur said:
The sound for the throat is Ah.
The sound for the heart is Who.

Richard McCann
(from Ghost Letters*)*

PIANO LESSON

My eyes open before the sun drops its yolk into the sky
and a girl upstairs is practicing scales. I imagine the arch
of her hand, the way her skirt might pause above the knee.

In the street I hear a victim, a paper cup, a man who talks
physics with a pigeon; a pair of girls blow bubblegum bubbles
at the sky. Perhaps an old woman dreams her childhood

on a park bench while the man beside her decides to leave
his wife. The world is complicated: an open window,
my head pressed to a pillow where I find a tidal action:

so many bodies rolling onto the planet, so many others
turning back. In a café I may someday light a cigarette,
remember the last person who did not love me, open my

mouth to see if it speaks smoke or words. But these days
I wake up wondering: how will I fit all this life in one life?
I need a map, a vocabulary list; I can't learn the world

fast enough. I want to be like the girl upstairs who has braced
herself before a grand piano and taught her own blind fingers to sing.

HOMECOMING

This was how I leaned, gently, against
a window: my eyes like the lightest
frost as my family sat down to dinner.

To see them from a distance was to see
a flock of birds unfolding in the sky.
I can't tell you enough of their tragic

beauty: the eager wings, the sounds
they made for love. I was standing
with a darkness which, like a cat,

might have eaten them whole but they
were blind to this. They were having
a holiday and even their dreams seemed

to come from a wind to the north. I can
tell you how a tree glowed behind them
and their gifts, unopened, longed to be

ripped. I can tell you how the darkness
melted away from me when I walked in among
them. Love sank deep as teeth or claws.

LUCK

Beneath the suburbs is a place to be late and wrong.
Plain and unlucky, I have visited many times.
Some days I feel a sinking towards that land
of blunders and my shirt turns to polyester,

my laugh goes so sharp it breaks bones. The first
time was a Halloween I spent with a distant cousin.
He is always in that under place: so drab even
mosquitoes overlook him. We spent the night

beside a silent phone, dressed as eggs, our hands
folded like bad cards. Once you've been under,
something shifts; you always go back. In recent years
I have gone there to miss trains, read maps

backwards, pay the rent twice and starve.
Sometimes I'm moving down a perfectly flat sidewalk
and falling. Once you've been, the other losers
are obvious: you see them knocking over

glass figurines, describing oral sex to the man
who cleans their teeth. They invite ten to dinner
and find themselves chewing alone. In a crowd
the unlucky throw the lucky off balance,

everyone's feet begin to squeak. When I was small
I loved a girl who gathered light by breathing;
her mouth was warm as sleep. Sitting close,
I would glow from looking at her, borrow shine

like a moon. My mother once explained:
we can't all be beautiful; even a gaunt field
feels the cold kiss of morning.

CHILDHOOD

When ancient Egyptians died the ones who survived them
said they had gone west. This is what my third grade teacher
told us in the dim light of a museum room lined with mummies.

I wanted to break the glass around each beautiful sarcophagus
and sing in the afterworld of the ones who lived before me.

Egyptians thought hard about the needs of the deceased and even
their bodies, so useless without life, were salt-dried and wrapped
in fine linen for the journey. In the afterlife Egyptians were heavy

with treasure, books, sometimes whole pyramids which,
my teacher said, was like vacationing with the kitchen sink.

I pressed my face to glass and believed I read the pictures painted
by hands since turned to dust. This was the story of a pharaoh
but I saw he was a child like any other. I could tell his parents

loved him: their faces drawn in profile, their arms crossed
like sticks. He had a pet cat and a pet bird and the cat was kind

while the bird was dark and unseen. One day the bird moved
over the pharaoh's bed and spoke its true name which was death.
The song of that bird has come down through the ages so I was

not surprised by notes light enough to reach my ears. That day
I entered the pharaoh's long-gone bedroom though my teacher

told me I was a child standing in a museum. Later that year
my teacher, caught stealing dresses, would hide from police
by flying, so quietly, to the west.

ENTROPY

My mother's kitchen was asleep.
Our family didn't gather there:
we lived and ate in our bedrooms
hypnotized by the blue lights of TV.
But, in her kitchen, pots and pans
floated, belly up, in the week-old
water, and our garbage, smiling,
outgrew its bag. All of this very

slowly, as if in a dream. My mother
despises what can never truly
be done so she does not care for cooking
or cleaning. If one cooks a fine dinner
one must wash the dishes to cook
a fine breakfast to wash the dishes
to cook a fine lunch and so on. My mother
explained this one afternoon in the basement
where the laundry grew around us like trees.

Our jungle-home was a metaphor for
my mother giving in to entropy.
When wine spilled on the couch and we
laughed as the stain unfurled,
we were embracing chaos. When we
fell asleep with the lights on
and the TV talking, we were
the weeds in our own garden.

My mother's kitchen was haunted.
Her refrigerator leaned to one
side and made only brown ice.
Her biscuits were as flat as plates.
But none of this mattered because
we were forgetting ourselves
even as we were becoming ourselves.
We pursued truth, beauty,
the meaning of life while

my mother's kitchen discovered
decay. All this unraveling—
moldy food, newspapers
piling up to the ceiling.
We loved each other like that:
bananas going black on the counter,
lines coming in around our eyes.

PUBERTY

When the school nurse came to us her hands
were damp as little clams. I still remember the movie
she showed: how the sperm flicked their tails
and the big egg seemed to laugh. Our bodies

were filled with the mystery of astronauts in places
we would never visit. When the nurse said erection
I saw a space shuttle and when she said blood I saw
the red rings of Mars. Scientists may have labeled

our parts but they said nothing of the shooting stars
each time the right boy reached for my hand. Sex Ed took
less than an hour that day but it was the subject
that exploded within us. One kid killed for it, some died

of it, and others—quiet as light—visited the forbidden
planets and came back weightless with wonder.

RUINS

The first one was in Michigan and I loved him
   like I was digging in a foreign land and he was
      the ruin I came to discover. Michigan is as cold

as people imagine and when I remember him now
   he is leaned against one of those gaudy American
      cars, big as boats, and all but his face is lost

in layers. This was a campus full of kids in knickers
   and baby blue sweaters who, when they laughed, shielded
      their mouths with mittened hands. I longed to uncover

flesh the same way I longed to uncover earth in a place
   where winter long outstayed its welcome. I wanted
      my beauty, whatever it was, held up to my blind eye

and described; I thought loving was the same as
   sifting down through ash to find Pompeii. In Michigan
      there were layers of snow and layers of clothing

and with that first boy it was as if I kept undressing
   until I was naked but I found a way, that young, to take
      off more. Down in the dirt of each other every clue we

uncovered was not enough. The snow did not stop falling
   and now, a decade later, there is the shape of him outlined
      again and again until he is larger but less detailed:
         a relic from the ancient landscape explaining me.

THE OWL QUESTION

White night fills the forest of my life: I am traveling in disguise.
This week I am myself the way my lover would like me to be:

smiling like I've seen life's meaning floating on a fat balloon,
talking false prophesies better than the men who made the emperor

nothing, then called it clothes. I am altered by every person who
loves me with ifs—if only I were myself but not myself, if only

we were the sort of lovers who felt passion the way oysters
feel salt water (an opened mouth at the full growth of the moon,

our hearts timed by one tide). I'm walking on ice and the dress
I wear is the weight my sister likes best; my hair is after

a Monet painting. Wherever I turn I am walking in the clear prints
of another person. I am rarely alone so this big-tree silence

surprises me: it asks the question owls have pondered for years.
Surely I am pure beneath the layers I've grown for love. I am

as honest as any animal with an arched back, a sigh, a new camouflage.

WHAT I LIKE

Not the party itself—a flurry of uncomfortable moments—and laughter
that really means something else. Not the moment just after the party
is over when we fall onto the sofa, dishes scattered everywhere,
cigarette butts floating in soda, a single untouched piece of pie

on the coffee table. What I like is the day after the party: the signs
of guests mostly erased, balloons tied to the pantry but flying
a little lower. The leftover food mummified in the fridge. I like
remembering that the room was full without standing in a full room.
Silence pours in like water and I swim alone: a fish in an empty aquarium.

RESCUE

My mother tells me how she wanted to save the iguana.
At home, by herself, she heard the ocean reaching to lick
her face. And above the trees, in a cottage with flamingo legs,
my mother saw how all her children had finally turned

to fish, waving her away with sleek tails like scarves.
In our absence, these long years while we swim, my mother
dreams of eggs swelling in the oven, of bread that will
never rise; she can't remember when the iguana first took ill.

She says he was our pet, not hers. She tells me how she came
to him with food he could not swallow and held it tight
against his tongue. He had glow lamps, an exotic oil
no one can know how she wanted him to live. Some nights,

in strong winds, the iguana watched my mother knit sweaters
no fish could move in. He licked his two teeth, told her
every pecking loop she made was perfect. The iguana liked TV
until his fever set in. He liked my mother's restrained laughs

like hiccups. I imagine them together the moment he died:
my mother wrapping him in layers like a mummy

giving him death with her love.

NUMBERS

An older woman told me how it was when her father died.
    We were in a diner beside Madison Avenue and the waiters

wore so much white she was reminded of heaven. The woman said
    she learned the news about her father then spent a year

adding figures. She had always disliked math and didn't know
    why she multiplied her rent by her dental bills but found

herself doing this all the time. She wrote her salary at the top of blank
    pages, circled in red ink: a tired eye. I looked down at my nicest

dress which was worn at the bottom like an old curtain. I thought of
    my grandfather who lived across the street from his parents until

he was seventy and they were ninety. Each morning he looked through
    his kitchen into the big window of his parents' living room.

At a certain hour, each day, his father lifted the curtain on that window
    and tied it back like hair. This meant his parents were awake and well

and a new day had begun. Of course there was the day when the curtain
    did not lift and many other days afterwards when my grandfather

stood alone in his kitchen counting.

RETRIEVER

My father, in middle age, falls in love with a dog.
He who kicked dogs in anger when I was a child,
who liked his comb always on the same shelf,
who drank martinis to make his mind quiet.

He who worked and worked—his shirts
wrapped in plastic, his heart ironed
like a collar. He who—like so many men—
loved his children but thought the money

he made for them was more important
than the rough tweed of his presence.
The love of my father's later years is
a Golden Retriever—more red

than yellow—a nervous dog who knows
his work clothes from his casual ones,
can read his creased face, who waits for
him at the front door—her paws crossed

like a child's arms. She doesn't berate him
for being late, doesn't need new shoes
or college. There is no pressure to raise her
right, which is why she chews the furniture,

pees on rugs, barks at strangers who
cross the lawn. She is his responsible soul
broken free. She is the children he couldn't
come home to made young again.

She is like my mother but never angry,
always devoted. He cooks for his dog—
my father who raised us in restaurants—
and takes her on business trips like

a wife. Sometimes, sitting beside her
in the hair-filled van he drives to make
her more comfortable, my father's dog
turns her head to one side as if

thinking and, in this pose, more than
one of us has mistaken her for a person.
We would be jealous if she didn't make
him so happy—he who never took

more than one trip on his expensive
sailboat, whose Mercedes was wrecked
by a valet. My mother saw him behind
the counter of a now-fallen fast food

restaurant when she was nineteen.
They kissed beside a river where fish
no longer swim. My father who was
always serious has fallen in love with

a dog. What can I do but be happy for him?

INVITATION

The cab is a snake and she is inside its belly
    like a swallowed egg. A boy invited her home,
        to dinner, which left her hands so cold

she bought swaddled flowers. The floral package
    waits beside her thigh, on the seat, and each sharp
        turn stirs it towards a door where the twelve

Marigold mouths open and close. She knows the boy's mother
    will rip the paper around the buds and squint.
        Like many other offers this invitation came

in code and she is unsure of its meaning. She wants the dinner
    to be about hunger and flesh since her own flesh wants
        and wants and she could join the other guests

easily: eyes narrowed, tongue darting. But the dinner is more likely
    about love and chewing, about the moment when the father
        will open his spotted hands and ask her questions

like a God. She believes the flesh is only following the mind
    which makes its movements angelic. The mind is grey
        and unseen. If these streets were made of rippled sand

she might have left marks to reflect on, but there is no sense
    in looking back. Even in transit her body asks for heat
        and dreams: a love to move above it

like a sky. The body demands pleasure to starve off fear.
    She longs to leave the worry of living but has accepted
        an invitation. She imagines this is the way we all come to earth.

MATRIMONY

When I went to visit I was, for one week, his wife.
The house was small and well formed like it might
belong to a doll. Mornings, he went to work and, while
he was gone, I walked from room to room in search of
my brain. There was a dog that longed to be walked
or fed and most days I ignored him the same way

I ignored myself. On the third day, I had a fever
and I could feel that any word I might utter would
lose its meaning. At first I had been a fine wife—
spotless dishes, low-cut dresses—but I was shrinking
and soon I would not matter as much as the dog.

Whenever the phone rang it was not for me
and when the plumber came to fix the sink he asked
if my parents were home. Luckily, my husband came
back from his long day and uttered the words
"comfort" and "reason". He did not notice my small
voice or my boiled head and we smiled and smiled

like we wanted to blind one another with sharp
white light. I imagined I could try on wife like
a fake fur coat and the way I looked in it would
make me laugh. Instead, wife was like gaining
fifty pounds, all on my ass, or waiting for bad news

from a doctor. When a person pretends marriage
they are brought in from the wild and placed naked
in a cement cell. A popcorn-crunching crowd comes
close and stares. On the plane home I was served
dinner for one and, afterwards, my tray table stayed
in the forward and upright position. I found my brain:
on my head all along like a useless pair of glasses.

ENGAGED

This was the summer I folded shirts in a shop where the lights
were as bright as the flames of hell. I lived on an island off an island

and every village had an Indian name. It was June and, come October,
I would marry a man so many states away I could not remember

the heat of his skin. I thought of Indians when I accepted rides from
strangers: smiling my way into foreign cars, hoping foreignness

would bring me back to myself or open the box I kept drawing
around my life. Maybe an Indian reasoned this way when he offered

his hand to we who would rob him of everything? This was the summer
my friends stopped calling, by chance, all of them poor and out of love.

It seemed love was intended for no one: I could not remember a season
when I was lifted by its salt as if by an ocean. Each time the phone

rang the man I was months from promising my future to would
light up like a fire fly then, quickly, vanish into dark. I suppose

I wanted to hold him, as if in a mason jar, and watch the movements
of his wings. Nights, bodies of flies pressed against my bedroom

window, I looked for a name or a meaning to give anything. Why was I
born and why did I stand all day in a hot shop folding shirts? Who was

the man I agreed to marry? Why did I want him until I was raw
with wanting and why did I go on wanting long after I willed myself

to stop? Why did he never say he could not live without me? Why did he
never cry: his hands unable to reach my body, our lives so short?

I didn't know that marriage was a war for territory: families giving
up beloved children, the walk to the place you make home like a trail

of tears. When I was twenty-five I wanted love to save me: a costumed
dance and a name for the way I was related. I didn't know I would

never have a name for so many things that mattered, would never belong
to anyone other than myself.

AFTER THE WEDDING

Leaves on the lawn twist sideways
    in this white night wind and my parents,
        weary from days of standing, drop

their shoes to the floor like stones. Aren't the windows
    around us cold and gaping amid such change?
        Won't you kiss me in the empty dance hall

where blue balloons fall over us like rain? Four formal
    questions in the book that turns a family into trees:
        When did you come? Who did you meet?

Who did you make? How did you fall away? Answers
    come the way babies come: as kisses leave the lips,
        as hearts love, or cease to beat, and the world

is made different in a day.

LUST

Blue Friday I walk to the wine and cheese shop
in my sleep. I'm wearing pajamas and the man
behind the counter blows smoke rings at my eyes.
His cat crawls up from a cold cellar and the dust

in its fur is too blue to describe. All I want is
a pair of wine glasses and ruby kisses on my thighs.
Sex should be easy—what animals do, what we do

to forget our own end. In my dreams a wine and cheese
man leans across inches of pine to tell me why I feel
blind attraction. There's a world of wine and cheese,
he says, and his blue cat agrees—a place where faceless

couples lean together and savor the aged in human nature.
What could be more old fashioned than lust? I am the spider
killing her mate, the fish swimming from egg to grave.

Friday, blue Friday, even in my sleep I am awake with desire.

DESIRE

The act of standing, penniless, in a store
where one might buy the porcelain skin
of beauty, the hot flowers of love, or glasses
so strong they see the other side of death.
The moment when a lover's mouth begins its
descent into flesh: a butterfly into forest.

PANDORA

Maybe I am the box and all the life
I find myself in is Pandora.
When my husband recalls an old
college lover—out spins envy—
a green fly with long eyelashes.
And my paycheck cashed with ten
dollars left in the bank is greed:
a bright-eyed spider and her honey
web. Lust is a white rabbit
and sloth is a hippo
sleeping in mud. Hate is a snake

expelled from the ears like heat.
Greeks believed people were pure
before Zeus sent down Pandora
with her suitcase of miseries:
a visitor with too much curiosity.
I'm sure she was always here

and there was no lid to lift. Like Eve
she brought the human race what
we already had. I am skeptical
of gardens and golden ages. Pandora,
we are told, saved hope but I don't
believe this either. She was childish,
silly: a new bride. She swallowed hope
the way the young swallow expectation.
She needed to fit in. Hope swelled
in her belly—a seed—and was born
again in blood, without eyes.

THE POST OFFICE

I once met a woman who wanted to marry the mailman,
the milkman, or the tooth fairy in a large white house
where the wind always whistled through the windows.
I could tell she had touched all her teeth with her own
tongue, swallowed milk without chocolate powder,
and sent love poems to businessmen in Chicago. She knew

I knew the answer to her dreams and I said: when the mailman
passes on a sidewalk or smiles beside the ice cream parlor
ask him how many letters are love letters and how many times
he has carried words against his thighs. He hears the deep
sighs of envelopes even when he laughs. He wants
to place his hands inside everybody's mailbox.

THE UNEXPECTANT

"We have news," my husband says to his parents.
We're sitting in their living room, near a bay window,
and we're enveloped by heavenly white light.
"We're not pregnant," my husband announces,
"We've decided not to have a baby this year."

"That's fantastic," his parents say. They stand
and walk towards us, their arms opened like
the wings of great birds. I already have a certain
glow. "How do you feel?" everyone asks me and
I smile. "A little nauseous," I say, "but mostly
alright." My husband's father asks what we
will name it. He is tall and gentle and he places

his hands in his pockets like a child. "We'll
have to wait and see how it doesn't look,"
my husband says, "There's so much of
nothing ahead." A few months later, there is

a shower in our honor. I wear a striped bathing
suit. My husband wears a thong. "Here are
some things you won't need," the relatives say,
"We're so happy for you." We grin and glow
from all the attention. We admire our shiny

new crib, our stroller with detachable car seat,
our rattle, our lifetime supply of pampers.
"Who do you suppose it will look like?" an aunt asks.
"No one we know," my husband assures her.
"Do you think you're ready?" my mother asks.
"Its hard to feel prepared," I say, "So much is unknown."

Everyone nods and I serve a very sweet cake.
It is chocolate with strawberry icing and there
is a picture of the future on top. In the picture,
we are all old or sick or dead and there is a blue
sky overhead. The world goes on without us.

Six months later, we drive to the hospital and sit
in the waiting room smoking an expensive cigar.
We watch some nurses try to revive a man
who has swallowed a bottle of aspirin. He has
white hair and his hands are thick and twisted
like roots. "I feel as if we've been waiting forever,"

my husband says. I tell him to think of how
I feel. Twenty hours later, nothing happens.
We call our parents from the hospital.
"We have news," we say, "We have given birth
to nothing." We all weep together, into our phones,
our puffy faces wet against the receivers.

The next day, everyone comes to our apartment
to have a look. I carry nothing in my arms.
It feels light and heavy all at the same time.
"Our future," my mother says. Her eyes fill
with salt water. The nothing is helpless
and unformed: I feel a deep burning in my heart.

OUR STORY

We hate the future in early fall.
You are worn and I am sorrow
if sorrow is a woman who cannot see.
Tell me our story. Were we perfect

at seventeen? Did we make love
in a hotel shower while someone
nearby knocked and pleaded into
the night? Did you visit New York

in mourning? Did we meet on a
train platform where men folded
newspapers and buildings leaned
together like lies? Was it like that?

Did we whisper while the elevator
went down? Did we leave our clothes
on a Cape Cod dune then remember
a low-flying plane? Did we marry

and move to a cottage by the sea?
So much of the story already told.
The dresses I wore; the expressions
you wore. Our pictures in a box

in the closet. Who could blame us
for refusing to write the rest? Somewhere
there will be trouble, somewhere
an unhappy ending. Inevitably, an ending.

THE NAME OF A FISH

If winter is a house then summer is a window
in the bedroom of that house. Sorrow is a river
behind the house and happiness is the name

of a fish who swims downstream. The unborn child
who plays the fragrant garden is named Mavis:
her red hair is made of future and her sleek feet

are wet with dreams. The cat who naps
in the bedroom has his paws in the sun of summer
and his tail in the moonlight of change. You and I

spend years walking up and down the dusty stairs
of the house. Sometimes we stand in the bedroom
and the cat walks towards us like a message.

Sometimes we pick dandelions from the garden
and watch their white heads blow open
in our hands. We are learning to fish in the river

of sorrow; we are undressing for a swim.

MAGIC

I learned the secrets from a dark smelling
book in the old country. I know the shape
of wild geese in the sky of my dreams
means I will marry more than once. Should rain
fall on a blue summer day and the shower
is over even as it begins this betokens
the luck of a fox's wedding and any wish

I make will come true. I know the new moon
is the Bride's moon, the full moon is Druid,
the old moon brings the Nights of Morgana:
a darkness, a time of no magic. If I want
answers I can slice, blindly, a pair of white
ribbons or I can lie down among the owls.

I believe in teacups speaking in leaves,
in dreaming cakes made on St. Faith's Day,
in the wisdom of Dove's eggs and early
tulips. Years before my birth my mother
fasted all Midsummer's Eve and, at night,
lay a lace cloth near a window. She spread

bread and ale on a plate and opened
a screened door to the wind. I came into
the room: her future daughter, her one
true love, and the toast we drank was
to a mutual unknown. Later, in a hospital,
under lights and drugs, my face swam

towards hers like an eel's and she said
she would have known me anywhere. I was not
raised in the thin pews of a church. I do
not cross myself or fall to my knees
with sin; bible stories are too bloody
for my liking. But I have loved superstition,

old wives' tales, any card or potion
that pretends to tell the truth. I know
the truth is anyone's guess: a white shirt,
if you will, placed on a tree limb before
a fire. On St. Mark's Eve, as the dusk
closes in, and the dew falls over a nearby
garden, lift your eyes and watch the arms
of the shirt. You will say they are moving,
talking, magically assuming a shape—
the shape of wind, perhaps, or a life.

FROGS

In the winter of my third grade year five men stood
at the door of my classroom holding forty buckets
of frogs. The frogs were dead and soaked in formaldehyde
so they looked like wet vegetables dug up on some

other planet. The girls around me let out a low moan of disgust.
Our teacher, Mrs. Winslow, was an oddity: a juvenile diabetic
who liked mini-skirts and clove cigarettes—sometimes she shot

insulin into her thin arms in front of the class. She had decided
we needed the frogs to teach us what went on beneath the skin;
she liked to shock. I remember the look of pleasure on her face
when the men placed the buckets, in rows, near our desks.

I was a child so I was curious and not afraid. I did not mind
the smell of the frogs or the fact of their death and I smiled
when I sliced open the thick skin on their backs. Our teacher

said we should learn the way things are made: that, in life,
we should take the unknown apart and break it down until
we understood what it was. This was not bad advice. Of course
this teacher did not last long—we were her first and last students—

so it was important that we remember what she said. There were
times when she stood before us, weeping, and read poetry
from other centuries we could not understand. Once, at mid-day,
she walked us into the school yard and whispered "go free":

we heard but could not move. For her I held my frog
without flinching and cut each tiny organ from its body.
And because of her I have taken my life apart many times,
to examine it, though I have never understood what it was.

COUNTING

I spent the first years of my life in the most
delightful coma: unable to count money
or read clocks. How telling this early idiocy
really was. In second grade my teacher discovered
the quarters in my pocket meant no more to me

than the pennies and this sent her into
a fury. What planet had I been sleeping on?
If only she knew. Where I lived, neighborhood
cats gathered for tea and trees spoke
a language as quiet as dew. I imagined my own

growth this way: my knee filling the space
where my head had once been. Snow, a miracle
I'd never seen, was two parts cloud and one
part dust. Of course, my parents were determined
to instruct me. They opened a card table

in the living room near a window full
of sky and they covered that table with coins.
We spent hours together leaned over our
neat stacks of dimes: I was their first child;
they wanted to do everything right. I felt

the penny should be worth more than the dime;
I got stuck on this point. I couldn't tell
the big hand from the little one on the clock.
I have never liked to measure—not flour

or milk—and certainly not something
invisible and unfriendly like time. Days came
and went. The light in my window was everything.
I caught a deadly spider in a jar; I learned to play
piano from an old woman I met in the street.

Sometimes, at night, I heard the clock
in the kitchen ticking. Sometimes my father
lifted me—his bird—over a restaurant counter,
enough money in my hand to settle the bill.

INNOCENCE

For Justin

Every summer there was a rented house
on the west side of town in a pastel shade
like a pale eye or a vein. And every summer
my two friends waited there: a brother and sister
so alike and in love they shared a lover:
a wild man painter who seduced them both
by washing their hair. The sister's hair was longer
and she told me how the painter did it
in a bathtub with cat paws—the water above

her like a sheet. The brother's was a baptism:
his flesh blessed in a sink. I learned first that anyone
can be anyone's lover. The brother and sister
took pity on me: I didn't know the world the way
they did. The sister led me through doll-sized
neighborhoods to find dresses in fat women's
garages because cloth was better if other bodies
had filled it. The brother said stepping into

the life of a mild housewife was worse
than waking up in a coffin. Every idea my southern
mother filled me with rose on my skin like a sweat.
The sister left her body easily: in her sleep, at work,
for full half-hours; she returned with stories like
dark photos. She thought her hands were someone
else's: she didn't know how to own them.

I was afraid then and I am still afraid now.
I was seeing all the ways I could fill the world
and I saw I could be anything: obscene, wrong,
another person's idea of perfection. The brother
and sister belonged only to themselves.
They flourished like untended gardens: big-vegetabled
beauty in a full head of weeds. It was a way of

getting older to know the sister really did leave her
body, for good, on a car ride that went blue as sky.
And the brother, lonely, crossed his arms and went
limp; he got a better job than he wanted, moved
to a city, worried he'd had too many lovers. I don't
know what this means. I want to be younger.
I want the sister to teach me how to feel my body
more as a dress than a skin. I want the hope I had
then: my hands unfolded, my thoughts
like a mazed rat's, the world turning its face
to me, and the face feeling wide and unhinged as a grin.

THE SINKING

I am bent over a sink of heavenly suds
   my hands moving like angels in wind

when I find myself weepy with work I will never
   make done. Beside me a garbage bag opens

and fills like some hungry lung and my newest shoes
   wear the fine lines of age. Even as I gaze

at the just-folded laundry I am seeing the first shirt
   I will open the way a diver opens water.

As a child I wondered at my mother's lost days
   in the polite lines of banks and supermarkets:

her head bowed as if in grief. Later I read we each lose
   years looking for lost objects and waiting for red lights

to change. One third of our earthly time passes on in our sleep.
   After one bill is paid another moves close like an enemy.

It's no wonder cavemen left only their own bones
   and a few reddened sketches of the hunt. My life story

is a series of telephone bills paid too slowly and dental visits
   for cavities I can't feel. Have I mentioned the car tags

I lost in the couch while kissing? They seem such a waste—
   these days I barely remember—doing the work that has no

meaning, the work that will whirl on above me when my body
   has crossed its arms to everything

and dirt loosens and falls into my heart like rain.

WILL

In grade school an unattractive girl I knew
distributed a questionnaire to our class:
she had decided to change herself. She wanted
our opinions on the most flattering hairstyle,
the sort of clothing she should buy.

I remember being impressed—not by the
questionnaire—which was simple and dull,
but by her willful desire for change:
she saw she was one thing and she wished
to be another. I have never had such clarity

of vision. Is every caterpillar also a butterfly?
Does the tadpole feel its fate on land? I am the one
with her back turned against change because
change is death whether it disguises itself

with a hat or a smile. That girl in grade school
took everyone's advice. She was a smart girl,
I'm told, and she made something of herself.

MY PORTRAIT

For Nana

My grandmother hired a photographer to make
a portrait of me before I went to school
because I was the first grandchild and because
she and I are tied together by chatter
and flower beds and southern manners.

She spent a week teaching me Mother Goose
nursery rhymes until I chanted perfect couplets
about babies falling from cradles and children
dying of plague and this convinced her
of my genius. The portrait was lavish:

I sat in an oversized velvet chair, the top
of which spread out like a fan, and a thin
yellow dress rested just above my knees.
My arms and legs were lean and crossed
and my face—which was the face of a pretty

child who has too often gotten her own way—
was smiling, but only a little. For many years,
my grandmother kept this portrait in her living room.
She sat across from it and smoked and read
and recreated my childhood: a time before

her husband died, a time when life was sweet
and dry like wine. She lived with the portrait
while I walked away from it: out of the south,
away from my youth; I called this getting educated.
She waited for me, the way the older generation

does. She waited for my return—to myself,
to her, to long iced-tea afternoons beneath
the trees. At twenty-five I married and,
that Christmas, she gave the portrait to my
husband. She said she was ready to part

with the me she knew then. My husband,
eager to know another me, hung it on
our bedroom wall. At first the portrait's presence
depressed me: I looked upon my well-made
younger self and saw that I should have been

so much more. I hated the weak face time
had etched for me: I wanted the long lean looks
of a child. Then, this morning, as if a fever
has broken, I have realized I am someone new
every time I open my eyes. I was someone

else a few minutes after that portrait was made
and, again, someone else days later. We are all
walking away from the beginning and towards
the end. My portrait is of
someone else, some other child.

FIELDS

For Henry and Irene Spruill

My great grandfather had some fields in North Carolina
and he willed those fields to his sons and his sons
willed them to their sons so there is a two-hundred-year-old
farm house on that land where several generations
of my family fried chicken and laughed and hung

their laundry beneath the trees. There are things you
know when your family has lived close to the earth:
things that make magic seem likely. Dig a hole on the new
of the moon and you will have dirt to throw away
but dig one on the old of the moon and you won't have

enough to fill it back up again: I learned this trick
in the backyard of childhood with my hands. If you know
the way the moon pulls at everything then you can feel
it on the streets of a city where you cannot see the sky.
My mother says the moon is like a man: it changes

its mind every eight days and you plant nothing
until its risen full and high. If you plant corn when
the signs are in the heart you will get black spots
in your grain and if you meet a lover when the
signs are in the feet he will never take you dancing.

When the signs are in the bowels you must not plant
or your seed will rot and if you want to make a baby
you must undress under earth or water. I am the one
in the post office who buys stamps when the signs
are in air so my mail will learn to fly. I stand in my

front yard, in the suburbs, and wish for luck and
money on the new of the moon when there
are many black nights. I may walk the streets
of this century and make my living in an office
but my blood is old farming blood and my true

self is underground like a potato. At the opera
I will think of rainfall and vines. In my dreams
all my corn may grow short but the ears will be
full. If you kiss my forehead on a dark moon
in March I may disappear—but do not be afraid—
I have taken root in my grandfather's
fields: I am hanging my laundry beneath his trees.

FINGERPRINT OF THE VOICE

All my head was filled with, years ago, is lost now.
So why do I still see myself days after my childhood house
went up in blue flames? I was eight, maybe nine,
and I was walking home from school. I remember

the shape of the sand blowing over the dunes and the dance
my leathery shoes made moving over cracks in the street.
If I slide my hand into a pocket I feel the pennies and paper

folded like birds: the things I stuffed my clothes with then.
Maybe I remember the still day so clearly because it came
after a catastrophe, a burning, an event that gave my life form.

But this does not explain why I have lost the memory
of the blaze itself: my father walking through a melting
bedroom saying my name. I have lost the language

I used with myself, all those years, in my head. Once, my mother
scolded me for turning away from a photo of my ancestors.
Didn't I care about the ones who had gone down before me?

How could I tell her their black eyes were like packages
I would never open? I wanted what I still want—an impossible
history of the thing deeper than nudity or bone:

a fingerprint of the voice of the soul.

SUMMER

During colder months on that Carolina island we natives
lived in neighborhoods of abandoned cottages: each one
smelling of salt and scrubbed white by wind and sun.

As a child I walked the silent streets, ocean breathing
by my side, and imagined a different life for myself

inside each empty house. I reached into damp hammocks,
stared through windows, opened screened doors
to porches where rocking chairs moved as if in sorrow.

I played with toys summer children left behind: plastic buckets
and shovels, naked dolls half-buried in sand. Later, grown up,

I moved to another sea-side village, walked Cape Cod beaches
in winter—quiet salt wind—and felt my childhood move
around me like a flock of white birds. Most Octobers

I awaken like the townspeople in Sleeping Beauty's castle—
my hat still in my hand, months vanished like a night.

I am always waiting for summer: my lost season.

FLAT WORLD

It occurred to her, as things sometimes do, that a child might
    unfold in the dark salt of herself like an oyster's pearl.
This was the way the world kept its stomach full—some woman,
    fertile as an ocean, growing ripe. There was a graveyard

on her street and the dead buried there were as old as cats.
    Stories could be gathered from the thin stones above
their slumber. Whole neighborhoods were formed by family
    plots and, even without bodies, the rich slept better

than the poor. Tombstones might have been houses
    with open windows for she could still glimpse lives
by looking in. One woman lost four children in two years
    then, the weight of babies like an undertow, died

giving life to number five. Her husband married again
    and again as if he could not remember how to fall in love.
What moves the living makes the dead lie back. They do not
    dream of beauty and feasts and the light head of fame.

Cemeteries made her see that the earth was as flat
    as her ancestors imagined. Without warning her own generation
would step off into space and a grave was the last known
    land before the fall. There, the grass over their mouths

like a blanket, human drama went quiet. The six-fingered
    spinster could no longer be seen. Those who lusted felt
their breathing go slack: scandal could never outlast bone.

    She was pregnant and she sat down
        on the hill with the coffins inside and waited.

HUNGER

Afterwards, I worried she was hungry.
While she was inside me I ate too much—

dinners in rich restaurants, curries, pastas,
little pies. I ate slowly, cautiously: I was

never full. After a meal I liked to sit
with a book in a tub of water and feel her

eating too; she tugged like a fish on
a well-baited line. Sometimes she was quiet

then, awakened by flavor, her phantom
dance began. I couldn't identify her parts

tucked inside me like they were—
she was everywhere and nowhere: a baby

Houdini. But after I pushed her out
and the nurses made her clean and wrapped

her like a bouquet of flowers and I was
wheeled to the silence of recovery

I worried about her hunger. True, the nurses
had their bottles and my breasts

were filling like wine glasses but milk
was thin when compared with the things

we'd eaten before. I was tired but couldn't
rest thinking of her away from me

in the strange glare of the world
with an empty belly. What if I could not

be for her what I had been in pregnancy?
What if I was not warm or salty enough?

Could I stretch and steal, as my body had,
to make room for her? It was easier when

I could feed her by feeding myself. Pregnant
I had been both selfish and giving.

Now I was no longer her container.
When she suffered it was not in silence.

LOVE

You grew a heart right away
because you knew about chambers
and pumping and love. There
were months when the world saw
only me with a coat pulled close
to hide the beating of us. I couldn't
feel you moving though you moved
and you couldn't hear me speaking
though I spoke. We were blind to
each other: a potato and its earth.

BECOMING MOTHER

Nothing prepares a woman for the way she is
ruined: her body torn like paper, her heart
white with violent love. Not the movies they

show in childbirth class—no beauty just blood—
not the baby showers where women tell stories
as old as birds. Not a woman's own mother

who has repaired herself by forgetting.
In the months before birth the world
stands still; afterwards there is only motion.

CHILDBIRTH REVISITED

I wanted to watch myself give birth as my
husband did: talking calmly with the doctor
while he opened his scissors. Blood everywhere
my husband said and the doctor touched

his arm, told him it was always like that.
So many witnesses: the nurse with her
machine recording contractions like
Seismic waves, the one with the baby

warmer, another doctor who asked
my husband if we'd like to keep the
placenta. They all saw my body open,
saw what I was made of, held my

daughter before I did. I was stuck inside
the birth which was like not being there
at all. They spoke to me the way you
might speak to someone in trouble,

Someone a great distance away. Birth is
awful though, at the time, I claimed
it wasn't. I was confused: a girl too
long at a cocktail party and told

them, as I was being sewn shut,
that the night reminded me
of the flu. I felt embarrassed that such
a thing had overtaken me, grateful

it was over, heroic for denying
myself their drugs. I was mad at
the doctor for cutting me—even if
it was for my own good, mad that

they put me on my back to push:
I felt defeated like that. Everyone spoke
to my husband because he was smart
and clothed and not ripped to pieces.

Awhile later the room was empty
and someone came to wipe up the blood
and I was given a stale little breakfast
on a tray. There was light coming

in through a window because it was
morning now and the staff changed
so the people who saw my labor were
on the street in plain clothes doing

ordinary things. One year later
I can still see their faces, still smell
the room where my daughter broke
free of me like a bird lifting

from the limb of a great tree.
My body was stunned by emptiness—
It was weeks before I stopped
reaching to feel the ripple

of her motion. During the last days
of my pregnancy I could smell her
through my skin: a creature so sweet
and warm I am still hungry

when she leaves the room.

OPERA

One day I made her laugh.
Such a simple thing—my head
against her belly, my hair
in her small hand. Her laughter

was like walking backwards in a field
of happiness. I tried all day to please
her; I wanted to know every inch

of the place she called pleasure.
The years of love letters
my husband and I mailed unfolded
like tongues in an opera.

ON HALLOWEEN

We dress our daughter in a flower suit
and carry her door to door. She can't eat
candy and doesn't know her name

but seems to understand the idea
of a holiday, a chance to travel in disguise.
She's quiet and wide-eyed: her hands

clasped in front of her green stalk.
Her petal crown is so yellow it might
be a halo. She senses her importance

in the doorways of friends' houses
where candy is dropped into paper sacks
and ghosts twist to sniff
the future in her new hair.

ASHES, ASHES

Winter is the death we have all been waiting for.
Even at parties where the new year is praised
branches are breaking beneath the weight of snow.
We know this season like we will know the end
of our lives when the living is halfway through.
Years go the way of childhood teeth: pressed so
hopefully beneath clean pillows. Dead skin.
The fingernails that grow without a pulse.

An earth that swallows babies
gives back a rash of white-eyed daisies.

SHOPPING

My husband and I stood together in the new mall
which was clean and white and full of possibility.
We were poor so we liked to walk through the stores
since this was like walking through our dreams.
In one we admired coffee makers, blue pottery
bowls, toaster ovens as big as televisions. In another,

we eased into a leather couch and imagined
cocktails in a room overlooking the sea. When we
sniffed scented candles we saw our future faces,
softly lit, over a dinner of pasta and wine. When
we touched thick bathrobes we saw midnight

swims and bathtubs so vast they might be
mistaken for lakes. My husband's glasses hurt
his face and his shoes were full of holes.
There was a space in our living room where
a couch should have been. We longed for

fancy shower curtains, flannel sheets,
shiny silverware, expensive winter coats.
Sometimes, at night, we sat up and made lists.
We pressed our heads together and wrote
our wants all over torn notebook pages.
Nearly everyone we loved was alive and we

were in love but we liked wanting. Nothing
was ever as nice when we brought it home.
The objects in stores looked best in stores.
The stores were possible futures and, young
and poor, we went shopping. It was nice
then: we didn't know we already had everything.

ALONE

When I was younger I loved until I disappeared.
I rested my head in my hand and saw only
the beloved: his unruly words, the chocolate
of his eyes, each hair on his head a vine

from the soul. If we were sitting at a table—
the other people around us, the table itself,
the light and sound of the place where we ate,
my own hand, even my breathing

melted away. Alone in my bedroom,
I often felt love a second time. I pressed my palm
to my ribs and fingered my heart. Sometimes
my body was as foreign as a stranger's.

I filled the silence of sheets and pillows
with myself. My thoughts, the weight of
my hair in my hand: the room was colored
by this. It has taken all these years to feel

myself and another at the same time. Even so,
a fascinating speaker at a cocktail party
will narrow my range of vision. My husband's
face against a pillow has caused whole rooms to collapse.

SPRING FEVER

It's not a real illness: my white-knuckled
mother could even see that. I might be learning
chess, another language, some skill to make
me rich. Instead I've gone stupid and high
as the thin breathless clouds. The saddest

thoughts won't bring me back to this world.
I dream of oceans and gulls: I'm on a red roof
drinking Margaritas and the sun is deep
in my skin, my bedroom hot thighs, long
after its licked the sky. I need this:

winter has sharpened its clear teeth on
much more than my boots. At night I undress
so slowly it's another day. At work I faint
while enlarging an article. I see boys blooming
in a field where the wind knows only

my name. I'm talking about sky-filled songs
in canoes without paddles, finding myself
on a picnic where the wine is free and sex
turns everyone to swans. I want the world
to love me careless and blinded. I want to lose

my fear in a season of parties: confetti on my face,
all life's finite hope leaning closer for a kiss.

ABOUT THE AUTHOR

FAITH SHEARIN WAS A FELLOW AT THE FINE ARTS WORK CENTER IN Provincetown and writer-in-residence at Interlochen Arts Academy. Her poems have appeared in journals like *Ploughshares, Chicago Review, Poetry Northwest* and many others. She has worked in a taffy store, interviewed elk hunters, read tea leaves and taught high school English. She earned her MFA at Sarah Lawrence College. She lives with her husband and daughter in Baltimore, where she is a visiting writer at American University.

THE MAY SWENSON
POETRY AWARD

THIS ANNUAL COMPETITION, NAMED FOR MAY SWENSON, HONORS HER AS one of America's most provocative, insouciant, and vital poets. In John Hollander's words, she was "one of our few unquestionably major poets." During her long career, May was loved and praised by writers from virtually every major school of poetry. She left a legacy of nearly fifty years of writing when she died in 1989.

May Swenson lived most of her adult life in New York City, the center of poetry writing and publishing in her day. But she is buried in Logan, Utah, her birthplace and hometown.